# DORSET BARNS

# DORSET BARNS

text **JO DRAPER**

photographs **DAVID BAILEY**

THE DOVECOTE PRESS

*Dedicated with gratitude to*
*Mark Watson (surgeon), his team,*
*the colorectal nurses and all the ward staff at*
*Dorset County Hospital*

A plain small barn, perhaps of cob, at Frome House, West Stafford, in 1816, drawn by Humphrey Repton. In the suggested landscape improvements, the barn is swept away to reveal views and the widened river. This didn't happen, but barns were clearly not seen as decorative.
Barn probably eighteenth century.

First published in 2010 by The Dovecote Press Ltd
Stanbridge, Wimborne Minster, Dorset BH21 4JD

ISBN 978-1-904-34987-7

Text © Jo Draper 2010
Photographs © David Bailey 2010

Jo Draper and David Bailey have asserted their rights under the Copyright, Designs and Patent Act 1988 to be identified as authors of this work

Designed by Little Toller Books
Typeset in Monotype Sabon
Printed and bound in Singapore by KHL

All papers used by The Dovecote Press are natural, recyclable products made from wood grown in sustainable, well-managed forests

A CIP catalogue record for this book is available from the British Library

1 3 5 7 9 8 6 4 2

# Contents

# Introduction

Despite many demolitions, Dorset still has hundreds of barns, in fact probably well over a thousand. They were a vital part of agriculture until the later nineteenth century, the largest buildings on the farms.

Barns were needed to store sheaves of corn, and for processing them. Josiah White recalled his father's barn at Whitecliff near Swanage in the mid-nineteenth century:

> The Great Stone Barn east of the house was an immense building. It had a doorway on either side large enough to permit the big wagon-loads of wheat to be hauled inside and unloaded. This barn held all the wheat from the farm. The bundles of wheat were stacked high at either end, the centre being the threshing floor where the grain was threshed out with flails.

He explains all the features of barns – the immense size to store the whole crop; the big doors (usually with porches) to accommodate wagons; and the threshing floor through the middle, lit by the doors. White continued:

> But our old barn has disappeared as I discovered when on a visit here in 1909. It was no longer needed for threshing machines can now do in a few days what was then an all Winter's job.

He is recording one of the greatest changes to farming – mechanised threshing of grain. From the earliest times until the mid-nineteenth century wheat was threshed by hand, the grain beaten from the ear by men wielding hinged sticks called flails. This was done on the floor of the barn, and as he says, usually took the whole winter. Simple hand-driven threshing machines started to be used in Dorset in the 1820s, and were part of the reason for the 1830 agricultural riots – labourers were worried about losing all their winter work.

*Opposite page* A barn in the middle of the village of Studland, with its porch opening onto the street. The cottage could possibly be a conversion of part of the barn: porches are usually in the middle of barns, not right up one end. Photograped here during the 1940s: both the barn and cottages have since been demolished. The barn is difficult to date, maybe eighteenth century.

Barns were a combination of store for the cut sheaves of corn, and the place for the long hard work of separating the grain from the straw. William Saint described the threshing at Dole's Ash near Piddletrenthide in the mid-later nineteenth century:

Thrashing with the flail was expert work and very hard work too. The men were stripped to the shirt in the coldest weather. They made their own flails and worked in pairs.

The thrashers placed the corn in straw [sheaves] on the floor and made a ridge across the floor. The two men faced each other and commenced whopping. Whop, whop, whop, their flails coming down one after the other in almost the same place, yet never touching.

. . . they thrashed the whole ridge flat, then without the slightest warning the flails were turned sideways and came up one on each side of the flattening ridge until the straw was in a ridge again, and then without the slightest pause the flails went up and down again, whop, whop, whop, all across the floor.

The men would be at New Barn more than a mile away from their homes from before daylight, and remain as long as they could see at night. They would take a bottle of cocoa, a piece of bread, and a bloater, or a piece of cheese for their breakfast and dinner.

The sheaves had been cut in the field with a scythe, bound into sheaves (great bunches) which were stood upright in groups to dry, and then carted to the barn for dry storage. Over the winter the grain was threshed out and sold to be ground into flour for bread, etc.

William Barnes is regretting the early threshing machines in *Eclogue: The Common a-took in* of 1834:

> Why here were vourteen men, zome years agoo,
> A-kept a-drashen half the winter drough;
> An now, woone's drashels be' n't a bit o'good.
> They got machines to drash wi', plague teake em!
> An' he that vu'st vound out the way to meake em'
> I'd drash his busy zides vor'n if I could!
> Avore they took away out work, they ought
> To meake us up the bread our leabour bought.

The 1820s hand-powered threshing machines were used inside the barns, and although they were quicker than hand threshing, they were not very fast. It was the invention of the steam traction

*Above* Barn in the farmyard at Dole's Ash Farm, Piddletrenthide. Drawn about 1900, this large barn was mostly timber, with a huge thatched roof. Since demolished.

*Below* The porches of the seventeenth century barn at Renscombe, Worth Matravers, like the one Josiah White described.

engine in the 1860s and the huge numbers available from contractors from the 1870s which made barns as corn-processing centres redundant. Contractors travelled traction engines with threshing tackle round the county, taking a couple of days to thresh a farm's whole harvest. It was much easier to store the corn in thatched ricks in a yard, where the traction engine could set up with its large threshing machine. The sheaves could be fed straight into the thresher, rather than having to cart them out of the barn.

That was the end of the real need for barns, although some were still built, and existing barns were used to store all sorts of things – even straw after the thresher had done its job.

The number of barns in an area depends on the amount of corn grown and the ability of the landowners to pay for them. Parts of Dorset have very few barns – the Blackmore Vale for example, where there has never been much arable. Generally there were about five farms to a parish, and each of these needed at least one barn. Small barns were needed by smaller farmers, and also by

*Above* The eighteenth century barn at West Stafford photographed in about 1895, when it was still a vital part of the farmyard.

*Below* Isolated field barn at Bradle, Church Knowle (early-nineteenth century), like William Saint's New Barn where the threshers worked.

*Above* Barton Farm barn, Cerne Abbas. The earliest Dorset barn (*c.*1350) and one of the barns Thomas Hardy used for *Far from the Madding Crowd*.

rectors who farmed their glebes and had to store their tithes when they were taken in corn and other produce.

The mad playwright John Pennie was fond of contrasting his own times (the early-nineteenth century) in Lulworth, with the eighteenth century, and he liked 'barns - those good old storehouses of plenty, of which there were once twenty-five in the parish; but in this age of finery, improvement, and poverty, there are not four now remaining.' Pennie liked to exaggerate: 25 barns in one parish does seem a high number and four a low one.

At the peak, probably in the mid-nineteenth century, there may have been more than three thousand barns in the county, large and small.

After the corn was threshed out, barns were emptyish until the next harvest. They were then big, convenient empty spaces used for many things, as Thomas Hardy shows in *Far from the Madding Crowd*:

They sheared in the great barn, called for the nonce the Shearing-barn, which on the ground-plan resembled a church with transepts. It not only emulated the form of the neighbouring church of the parish, but vied with it in antiquity. . . . The vast porches at the sides, lofty enough to admit a wagon laden to its highest with corn in the sheaf, were spanned by heavy-pointed arches of stone, broadly and boldly cut. . . . The dusky, filmed, chestnut roof, braced and tied in by huge collars, curves, and diagonals, was far nobler in design, because more wealthy in material, than nine-tenths of those in our modern churches. Along each side wall was a range of striding buttresses, throwing deep shadows on the spaces between them, which were perforated by lancet windows, combining in their proportions the precise requirements both of beauty and ventilation.

One could say about this barn, what could hardly be said of the church or the castle, akin to it in age and style, that the purpose which had dictated its original erection was the same with that to which it was still applied. . . . Standing before this abraded pile, the eye regarded its present usage, the mind dwelt upon its past history, with a satisfied sense of functional continuity throughout – a feeling almost of gratitude, and quite of pride, at the permanence of the idea which had heaped it up. The fact that four centuries had neither proved it to be founded on a mistake, inspired any hatred of purpose, nor given rise to any reaction that had battered it down, invested this simple grey effort of old minds with a repose, if not a grandeur, . . .

*Above* The huge and the small – Abbotsbury Great Barn and a smaller one (probably seventeenth century) at Studland Manor Hotel (converted into garaging). They performed the same jobs even though they look so different.

Today the large side doors were thrown open towards the sun to admit a bountiful light to the immediate spot of the shearers' operations, which was the wood threshing-floor in the centre, formed of thick oak, black with age and polished by the beating of flails for many generation, till it had grown as slippery and as rich in hue as the state-room floors of an Elizabethan mansion.

Later in the novel the Harvest Supper is held in the same barn:

The central space, together with the recess at one end, was emptied of all incumbrances, and this area, covering about two-thirds of the whole, was appropriated for the gathering, the remaining end, which was piled to the ceiling with oats, being screened off with sail-cloth. Tufts and garlands of green foliage decorated the walls, beams, and extemporized chandeliers, and immediately opposite Oak [the hero] a rostrum had been erected, bearing a table and chairs. Here sat three fiddlers . . .

The novel was written in 1873, and the wheat is not stored inside the barn, but in a stack-yard: 'There were five wheat-stacks in this yard, and three stacks of barley.'

The barn in the novel was a compendium of several Dorset

*Left* Sheep shearing in the barn at Turners Puddle in 1912, with one of the porches behind. The surface foreground is probably the thick wooden threshing floor. The shearers look tired – hand shearing with clippers was very hard work.

*Opposite page* Field barn on Chaldon Herring Down, dating from the late-eighteenth or early-nineteenth century.

barns, but Hardy told a friend he was out cycling with that it was largely based on Barton Farm, Cerne Abbas (see page 10).

Hardy sees the barn as an ancient but still vital building, and indeed we still think of barns as the epitome of rural life – all warm straw, happy chicken, and proper farming.

Bosworth Smith describes a subsidiary use for barns – in the mid-nineteenth century:

What joy it was, when we were children and the day was hopelessly wet, to be allowed to put behind us, for the time, the humdrum of everyday life, and transfer ourselves to the mysterious and awe-inspiring precincts of the barn! No other spot, not even the hay-loft, seemed so to fill our childish imaginations. When once the big folding doors had been shut behind us, we said good-bye to the outer world; we seemed to be in another world, a world of shadows. Such muffled sounds as managed to reach us from outside seemed to come as from very far away.

The rustle of the mouse or rat, coming nearer and nearer, filled you with half-fascinating awe, as though it were the footfall of some beast of prey in the Indian jungle. The venerable rafters seemed to grow in size, in the prevailing gloom, the darkness visible; the roof above them seemed to rise higher and higher, till it loomed on the imagination like the groined arches of some Gothic cathedral, and the yard-long cobwebs of the centuries which depended from it, seemed like the glowing ashes in a dying fire, to take weird, and, ever-varying shapes.

Children must have always played in barns, with or without permission.

Dorset's surviving barns come in every size and style, using every possible building material from cob (mud) to Portland Stone, with brick and timber along the way. Their dates range from medieval times up to today, and whilst some have been converted to housing and other uses, many are still at the centre of farming.

# Medieval Barns

Barns have been needed to store and process corn forever but the earliest barns do not survive. The oldest barns in England date from the thirteenth century, with two famous ones at Cressing Temple and another at Coggeshall, all in Essex. These still have their impressive original timber frames. Stone barns of the thirteenth century survive too, in the Cotswolds and other stone areas.

Dorset's six earliest barns were built by monasteries, and this tends to be true over the whole country. Monastic establishments assumed that their community would go on forever, so investment in buildings of high quality was only sensible. Strong and expensive buildings are the only ones to survive from medieval times.

These monastic barns were some of the largest medieval buildings, often as big and impressive as churches. Monasteries were abolished in the 1530s: the new owners of their lands still needed the barns, which were preserved even when the rest of the monastery was demolished.

The very earliest Dorset barn is at Barton Farm, Cerne Abbas, dating from about 1350. Like most of these earliest ones it has been shortened, lost its original roof and been altered. Here the alterations are spectacular: four bays were converted into a farmhouse with Gothicky windows. When it was sold in 1919 the agents enjoyed describing the 'HISTORICAL RESIDENCE, which has been taken from the Southern end of the splendid old MONASTIC BARN, and can be enlarged by the adoption of the remainder.'

Well, no-one took up that option, and the combined house and barn is still much as it was when sold.

In 1774 it was still all used as a barn, much admired in the first edition of Hutchins: 'a magnificent stone barn, which formerly belonged to the Abbey: and still receives the produce of the farm.' The 1813 edition adds, 'The old barn is built with alternate layers of free stone and chipped flints, very neatly disposed.' So it still is, with what one historian calculated as more than 170,000 worked

*Opposite page* The barn at Barton Farm, Cerne Abbas, of *c.*1350. The left hand end was converted into a house in the early-nineteenth century. Original porch centre.

*Left* The barn at Barton Farm, Cerne Abbas, engraved for the first edition of Hutchins *History of Dorset* (1774), 'on account of its size and stateliness'. The detail does not match the building exactly, but it gives a good impression of the barn before conversion. With both doors open, the way through looks like a road.

(knapped) flints facing its walls, inside and out. These very neat squared flints, set in straight courses, are unusual in Dorset.

Henry Moule lamented the conversion of the south end into a farmhouse 'knocking through the door and window openings is said to have cost almost as much as a new house would have done'. This must have been done soon after 1813. Moule visited in the late 1880s, and saw the original roof surviving in the house end – the barn end roof fell down in 1885. The rest of the roof followed soon after, but the original stone tiles were put back on the new timbering.

There are big porches either side, one with a small side door, sometimes called a 'last exit' door, used when the huge main doors had been barred for security.

Thomas Hardy cycled to Cerne with a friend in 1907, and admitted that this barn was 'one of the chief models . . . [for] the description of the barn' in *Far from the Madding Crowd*.

The barn was originally longer by another entrance and four more bays, which would have made it 172 feet long. The start of the arches for the entrances survive in the current end wall.

Henry Moule was curator of the Dorset County Museum and published a great deal on Dorset's history and archaeology. Earlier farming brought out the romance in him, and after explaining the detail of Barton Farm Barn in 1901 he asked his fellow visitors to imagine 'the millions and millions of sheaves which have been carted in great loads through this stately barn-porch. And what divers fashions of raiment on the farm-folk, grouped with red wheat-loads. Would this porch could utter speech and tell us

of some of the far-off harvest homes among the five hundred which it has seen.' Lovely that he recorded this building, and also imagined its use. In 1901 sheaves of corn were still being brought back from the fields in wagons, and manoeuvred by hand, just as they had been when the barn was built.

Abbotsbury is the one barn which cannot be ignored – huge and picturesquely set in the landscape. It has been admired since the eighteenth century, and its image has appeared on dozens of prints, hundreds of paintings and innumerable postcards, and even on a postage stamp.

It was built for Abbotsbury Abbey about 1400, and when complete it was the longest barn in the county, measuring nearly 300 feet. (Sadly there were several even longer in the country.) Originally there were 23 bays with only two doorways on each side, and three smaller doorways. The surviving porch is impressive – two storied with the staircase in a turret tucked into the corner externally. The upper floor even has a window.

Like Cerne, Abbotsbury can be dated by the arch to the porch, and its general style. The original roof is long gone. In 1859 it was noted that 'the contrivances for enabling persons to oversee every part of the building are curious and ingenious, and the gable end retains vestiges of its original beauty'. If only they'd described the security contrivances, but this a reminder that barns were secure storage against thieves as well as the weather.

By the early eighteenth century one end was roofless – an engraving of 1733 shows half with just parts of the walls.

The barn at Cerne has been partly altered into a house: Abbey

*Right* Gable end of Barton Farm with characteristic buttresses. One original slit, top. Windows inserted in the early-nineteenth century.

*Below* Detail inside the barn at Barton Farm, drawn by Henry Moule in the 1880s, showing the neat coursed flintwork (dark) with stone corners. The shovel is a wooden one for grain.

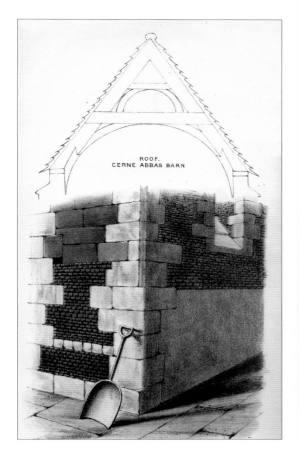

ROOF.
CERNE ABBAS BARN

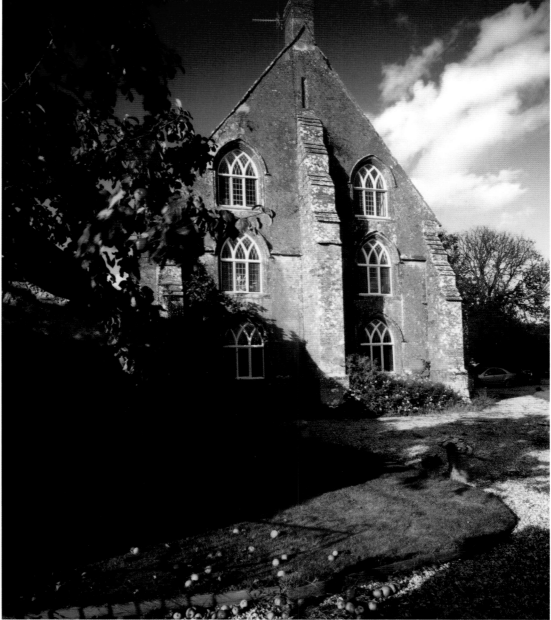

Barn, Sherborne has been even more violently adapted by demolition of the main parts of the barn, and the conversion of the area between the two porches into a house.

Abbey Barn was built in the late fourteenth or early fifteenth century for Sherborne Abbey, and was large. Hutchins records in 1815 'in the abbot's barton is a noble rag-stone barn entire, and still made use of. The timber roof the roof is a very curious piece of ancient architecture'. So it probably was, but in 1827 the barn was in poor condition, and both large ends were demolished to make the centre into a house, which from around 1900 has been the headmaster's house of Sherborne School.

Tarrant Crawford was a rich Cistercian nunnery, and one of its farm buildings survives with the oldest (late fifteenth century) barn roof in Dorset. Externally the building looks simple and

*The Tithe Barn at Abbotsbury, with the Abbey on the hill behind*, a watercolour c.1795 by Thomas Girtin (1775-1802). A little building tucked in beside the porch. The yard is lively with pigs, cows, a cart, and workhorses drinking: a reminder of how busy barns and their yards were when they were at the centre of farming.

18

low, if old. Alterations seem to have removed the characteristic barn porches, and perhaps the barn was originally larger.

The lower part of a 'proper' late medieval barn survives close by, and in 1774 Hutchins reported 'there was lately a large old barn here, which by its style of building was supposed to have been the abbey church.' Barns and village churches were often the same size and of the same materials, unsurprising to muddle them. (See page 20).

The fifteenth century barn at Corscombe was also monastic, built by Sherborne Abbey on one of its outlying estates. Along with Corscombe Court, the large farmhouse, it is still enclosed by a moat. The smallest surviving medieval barn in the county (Abbey Farm now Beauvoir Court) was also built by monks – at Cerne in the fifteenth century. This and Barton Farm barn are the survivors – Hutchins records that 'the old abbey house, many large barns etc. made out of the abbey, were burnt about 50 years ago' *i.e.* about 1720.

Most medieval barns have disappeared over time. Dorset is lucky to have these six surviving.

*Above* An engraving from Hutchins of Abbey Barn of Sherborne in 1815, before it was converted into a house. A narrow building alongside the porch once housed a stair for access to the room above. Now called Abbey Grange, the house is hard to match to the original. The barn has been sliced through, leaving only the part between the two porches (left and right). A new wall with its windows was inserted each side.

*Left*  The roof timbers in Tarrant Crawford, late fifteenth century. This is a hammer-beam roof – the horizontal beams sticking out from the walls are the hammer-beams. These are braced by arched timbers and the whole arrangement gives useful high space in the barn, because the roof doesn't have tie beams.

*Below*  Three barns at Tarrant Crawford by Rena Gardiner. Second left, the barn with fifteenth century roof (only the buttresses hinting at the early building externally); right, fifteenth century foundation with brick top of 1759; and centre, a twentieth century barn.

*Above* The barn at Corscombe Court, built in the fifteenth century with an impressive porch.

*Left* The roof of the porch at Corscombe Court, with big trusses (braced collar trusses), the purlins (thicker ones) spanning across them, and then the thinner ones, rafters. In barns all this is exposed because there are no ceilings.

A ll the big medieval barns in Dorset are called *The Tithe Barn*. This name generally comes in during Victorian times: most of them were called *The Great Barn* earlier.

The use of the phrase 'Tithe barn' is misleading, because the barns were not there just to take the one-tenth tithe of corn. Imagine what acreage would be needed to fill Abbotsbury 'Tithe' barn if it was only taking one-tenth of the produce (and indeed where were the other nine-tenths being stored and processed?).

In the 1880s, Henry Moule looked at Barton Farm, Cerne Abbas, which was starting to be called a Tithe barn. He knew that before one end was converted into a house 'it held all the corn in straw [sheaves] off a farm of 800 acres. Therefore, it would hold the tithe corn off 8,000 acres, more than 12 square miles' and he estimated that this would have stretched 6 miles up and down the valley giving problems transporting the corn. These were not tithe barns, but the barns for large monastic estates, taking *all* the produce, not one-tenth.

Real tithe barns were quite small, used by rectors for their tithe corn, and often for their own corn from the glebe land as well.

*Right* Swanage Tithe barn (seventeenth century), typically small, originally in the Rectory gardens.

*Below* The barn at Glebe House, Bloxworth (probably eighteenth century), with later repairs. The Glebe was land belonging to the rector, and this is what a good-sized tithe barn looks like.

*Left* The Abbotsbury Great Barn in 1733, engraved by Nathaniel Buck, with half the barn falling to ruin but half still in use.

*Below* The Great Barn at Abbotsbury today, still much as it was in 1733 with its regular buttresses and huge two-storey porch.

All the early barns have buttresses – little extra pieces of wall at right-angles to the main walling. These are very decorative, but that is not why they exist. They are carefully positioned exactly where the big roof trusses meet the wall, and are there to reinforce the wall against the thrust of the roof trusses.

Some later barns also have buttresses, but the later roof structures do not need them as much as the early ones do.

Very tall buttresses were used on the gable end walls: these do not relate to the roof, but to worrying about the stability of the high wall needed here.

All these original buttresses are bonded into, and neatly built in the same style as the wall they help to support, and usually of the same materials as the barn. Another sort of buttress, often in different materials, was added when a building was having problems. These are easy to spot because they look so separate.

*Above* The gable end of Abbotsbury today. The buttresses are all original – big double ones on the corners.

*Left* The barn at Tarrant Crawford shows the two sorts of buttresses – original stone ones, part of the wall, and added brick ones.

*Opposite page* Inserted brick buttress on a local stone barn at Bench, Portesham. It has done its job supporting the wall, while the rest of Stall Barn has disintegrated.

# Tudor Barns

Like medieval barns, most surviving sixteenth century barns are large, although there are a few very small ones. Barns were built by the big landowners who rented out the farms, or by the farmers themselves when they owned their land.

Forde Abbey built itself a large barn early in the sixteenth century, and the double barn at Wyke may also be monastic, but it is not closely dateable, and may have been built by the person who bought the monastic estates. Wyke is very impressive – two barns, end-to-end, measuring 230 feet, very plain apart from the buttresses. Sheer size gives them their character. Double barns, rather than one huge one, are not uncommon: it has been suggested that one would be used for wheat, the other for barley. Equally security may be an issue: policing a very large barn is more difficult than two medium-sized ones. At Wyke the roofs are a little different from each other, suggesting that they were not built at exactly the same time.

Ford Grange, close to Forde Abbey, was part of the monastic estate, and a large barn survives there dating from the early-sixteenth century, the very end of the monasteries. One end is full of holes for pigeons to nest in: these were for food, not ornament. Much of the original roof survives.

Hinton St. Mary has a large barn close to the Manor House, dating from the early-sixteenth century and built for the manor, not a monastic establishment. It had two huge porches, but these have been altered to make entrances because the barn was adapted into a theatre in the early twentieth century. This is one of the few Dorset barns to have a fireplace, with the most amazing over mantle, probably from Cerne Abbey and dating from the 1460s or 1470s, moved here in the early twentieth century. So Hinton St. Mary does manage a monastic connection.

All these early barns are large ones: at Woolsbridge the picturesque buildings include a small sixteenth century barn, much altered externally but still with its original roof timbers. Like many later barns in low-lying situations it is right on the road, so as to use the

*Opposite page* Ford Grange, Thorncombe. The gable wall (with ventilation slits) of this early-sixteenth century barn peeps through the nineteenth century farm buildings.

*Above* The early-sixteenth barn at Ford Grange, Thorncombe, typically with buttresses. Two big doors this side, and two porches on the other side The many holes for pigeons to nest are very neatly made.

relatively clean and hard road surface as a working area.

The barn at Winterborne Clenston is very picturesque, and has a strange building history. The chequered pantiles of the roof are Victorian. The walls are banded flint and stone, with a big porch either side, and date from the sixteenth century. The timbering of the roof, however, is at least 100 years older than the building, but must have come from a hall, possibly a monastic hall. Milton Abbey has been suggested, but Cerne must be possible too.

This barn has big porches either side, whereas most of the early ones only have porches on one side. These porches have little side doors which are 'last exit' doors, used when the big doors have been barred and bolted from the inside.

Sydling St. Nicholas has a huge sixteenth century barn (see page 34), built of flint and originally with a thatched roof. When

Frederick Treves saw the barn in about 1904, he noted 'the barn has, as is fitting, a heavy roof of thatch. Melancholy to tell, this is gradually being replaced by corrugated iron.' There was still some thatch in 1939, but its replacement is now complete now, and while Treves hated the corrugated iron, it has preserved the barn.

Unusually for Dorset, the barn is aisled inside, with huge oak posts supporting the roof structure set out from the walls. One of the beams of the roof had 'LVW 1590' carved into it, for Lady Ursula Walsingham. This date would fit the structure well.

The Sydling barn has been admired for a long time. When Emily Smith visited Sydling in 1836 she 'walked up to the large barn built in the reign of Queen Elizabeth. The floor and beams are of solid oak'. The solid oak floor was the threshing floor, set between the porches.

*Above* The barns at Wyke, Castelton, with the three porches rowing up. The black bags contain silage.

*Left* The typical sixteenth century roof at Wyke. The two straight tie beams running across are later inserts. The original roof has a heavy triangular frame reinforced at the apex, and very heavy purlins running the length of the roof. The curved pieces between the purlins are wind braces.

*Below* Looking along the barns at Wyke showing the big buttresses. The closer barn has two porches on the other side, with matching wide doorways. The further barn has opposed porches, one just visible here.

*Above* Barn at Baglake, Litton Cheney, built of local yellowy limestone and hard chalk (clunch), the really white upper walls. Like cob, clunch needs more solid foundation courses. Probably sixteenth century, but possibly later.

*Left* The early-sixteenth century barn at Hinton St. Mary, with its two original porches. In the 1930s the barn was converted into a theatre, and the roof extended down between the two porches. The windows and timbering date from the 1930s, as does the chimney.

*Above* Woolsbridge Manor, East Stoke photographed in 1934 with the original thatch and roadside porch intact.

*Above right* The complex of building materials in the Woolsbridge barn – flint, pale stone and very dark heathstone, thin stone on edge (herring bone) and on the top neat brickwork. Late-sixteenth century at the bottom, probably eigtheenth century top.

*Below* The small sixteenth century barn at Woolsbridge Manor, East Stoke today, with the Manor House visible behind.

*Above* The sixteenth century barn at Winterborne Clenston, banded flint and stone with unusual Victorian chequered pantile roof.

*Left* The fifteenth century timbering of the roof at Winterborne Clenston, with many of the timbers decorated with mouldings. This is a hammer-beam roof, and strangely the hammers (the short horizontal beams) are not decorated, suggesting that they may be replacements. The timbers are mostly supported on stone corbels. Oddly, the roof is at least one hundred years older than the barn itself and must have come from another building.

*Above* Close to the church in Hazelbury Bryan, this barn was altered at this end to form a stable, but inside the sixteenth century jointed-cruck roof survives.

*Left* One of the crucks at Hazelbury Bryan in the 1970s. The main beam supporting the roof is jointed into a vertical post which continues right down to the floor.

*Below left* A sixteenth century barn in trouble – Wytherston, Powerstock, catching fire in the late 1950s. This destroyed the roof, but happily after 60 years with a tile roof, the barn was carefully restored in 2009, and is now thatched with water reed.

*Below right* Small stone barn at Wych, Burton Bradstock, converted into a house about 1989. Characteristic stone finial on the gable end. Probably sixteenth century.

The sixteenth century barn at Sydling St. Nicholas was originally longer, extending beyond the porch on the right. Opposite this short porch is a much longer one. The gable end adjoins the churchyard, with neat ventilation holes and slits in the flint wall.

Inside the barn at Sydling St. Nicholas showing the original timber framing. Unusually the barn is aisled. The upright posts are joined with a heavy tie beam, braced underneath. Standing on the tie beam are short queen posts.

*Above*  The late-sixteenth century barn at Poxwell in the 1940s and today – it is difficult to see the porch now.

*Top left*  Reset in the sixteenth century barn at Poxwell is an earlier window, probably a hundred years older than the barn.

*Left*  Detail of one of the wooden trusses at Poxwell, showing the joint between the upper and lower parts of a cruck. The wooden pegs joining the two timbers show as little circles on the lower face of the timbers.

*Opposite page*  The roof of the late-sixteenth century barn at Poxwell, showing the jointed crucks. The main roof timbers are braced by collar beams towards the apex.

# Seventeenth Century

Seventeenth century barns tend to be complete, unlike the medieval ones which have ends knocked off *etc*. Several are ideal barns – chunky, of local stone, and almost timeless because they are so simple. Lillington is maybe the very best – larger than most, and plain. It was built about 1600, fronting straight onto the village street, and with matching big porches either side. There are three buttresses on the far side, but none on the front because the builders were happy that the roof and walls could cope without reinforcement. The original roof survives with no problems: they were quite right.

There may well have been barns with dwarf stone walls and wooden weatherboarding before the seventeenth century, but none survive. Buildings with wooden cladding are vulnerable if they are not well-maintained, so many have disappeared. Two seventeenth century barns with weatherboarding survive in Dorset. Tomson Farm, Anderson, still has the original roof trusses, and at Woodsford Farm (on mostly brick dwarf walls) the roof is of very unusual construction, with sling-braces. These were also used in the barn at Whitehouse Farm, Holnest, which had dwarf stone walls (see page 53).

Occasionally barns with cob (mud) walling survive from the seventeenth century, and again there were probably earlier ones which don't. If given a good pair of shoes (dwarf walls of stone or brick) and a good hat (usually a thatched roof) cob can endure very well, but if neglected it quickly deteriorates. The barn in Church Lane, Piddletrenthide, has walls that are two-thirds cob, with flint walling below and a few brick repairs.

Most seventeenth century barns are sensibly of stone, like the earlier ones. This is a more expensive way of building, but more durable than timber cladding or cob. Whitcombe has a perfect simple stone barn, set very prominently near the church in the tiny hamlet. It dates from the late-seventeenth century, and there is another, larger barn of the same date tucked in behind the house.

Chideock (see page 50) has three smallish barns all probably dating from the seventeenth century, all right by the road to take advantage of the hard standing offered. All are small, inevitably in an area where there was little corn grown, and all are in the orange local stone. Adjacent Symondsbury has more of these small but well-built barns.

*Opposite page* The barn at Lillington.

*Above* Looking across the church at Lillington with the barn beyond – about 1920. The barn looks at least as big as the church.

*Left* The barn (*c.*1600) at Lillington in 1939 still in use as a barn, and today after conversion into a house in the 1970s. The roof of Lillington barn is typical of around 1600 – a collar beam roof. The big vertical timbers are tied together towards the top with a short cross beam called a collar, and below are elegantly curved timbers (arch braces), making an arch and strengthening the joints. The smaller curved timbers are wind braces.

*Below* The early-seventeenth century barn in Church Lane, Piddletrenthide, in 1990, just before it was converted into a house. The upper walls are cob. The big doors to the porch are split in two horizontally as well as vertically: the upper ones are open in the photograph. The horizontal boards at the bottom are the cill or threshold, which kept animals out while threshing was going on.

*Above* Crowded farmyard at Toller Fratrum: the big barn along the back could be seventeenth century: it has been much adapted. One porch (left) is less altered. In front, an eighteenth century wooden granary on staddle stones to keep rats and mice out of the grain.

*Below* Large seventeenth century barn at Renscombe Farm, Worth Matravers, with two big porches and a modern slate roof. As often happens, there is a later building tucked in between the porches.

*Left* Yuill Farm, Friar Wadden, has a very plain seventeenth century stone barn with a rather small porch for its size.

*Above* The roof is surprising inside – a very modern steel structure running right to the ground, leaving the walls holding up nothing.

*Top right* Gable of a seventeeth century barn at Iwerne Minister, with a huge stepped buttress and diagonal buttresses at the corners. The barn is now housing.

*Top left* Another seventeenth century barn at Iwerne Minister. This one low and converted into cottages, but with all the buttresses surviving. The soft local Greensand makes the building look even older.

*Left* Very simple seventeenth century barn at South Bowood, Netherbury, probably built in the 1660s, but slightly adapted and repaired in 1813. These smaller barns tend not to have porches.

The seventeenth century barn at Tomson Farm, Anderson, with dwarf
walls in rubble stone, and timber weather-boarding above.

Inside the barn at Tomson – two original roof trusses background, arch-braced collar beam, and in front of it a modern truss, very square timbers, with a sort of king post.

*Left* Narrow porch at the far end of the barn at Silton, with later farm buildings encroaching on it. Unusually some of the porches and a gable end have wooden boarding in the upper parts.

*Above right* The gable wall at Silton, adapted in the lower part with a doorway and window. One ventilation slit has later been lined out with brick. Tall owl hole at the top. This wall is part of an eighteenth century extension to the barn.

*Below* The seventeenth century barn at Silton, very close to the Manor House one side, and this side the farmyard. Wide but shallowish porch on the eighteenth century extension.

*Above* The late-seventeenth century barn at Whitcombe after careful restoration in 2008, with its new thatch and wide doorway, but no porch.

*Below* The hamlet of Whitcombe in the 1920s, with one barn prominent centre, and a second barn visible left.

*Left* Seventeenth century barn at Carters Lane, Chideock, restored in 1845 (datestone top) and with a probably twentieth century sliding door. Loading bay above.

*Below* Carter's Barn, Chideock, with a cart-shed of unusual design attached, possibly added in 1845 but reusing old materials. This looks deliberately picturesque, but it is useful too.

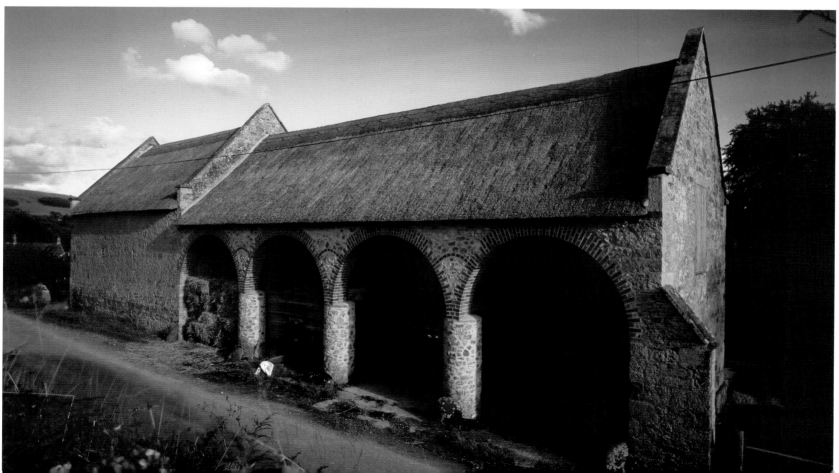

The ultimate in conversions – a smallish seventeenth century barn at Newton, Swanage, converted into one big room, a baronial hall, in the 1870s by Charles Robinson. Where the big barn doors were, he inserted a huge bay window (left). The fireplace (right) came from Tuscany, and is probably in the other big doorway.

The arrangements of the big timbers which support barn (and indeed all other) roofs follow the same sort of development all over the country. People wanted to use timber efficiently, but they also wanted as much clear space as possible inside the barn or other building. The most efficient structure for roofs is the simple triangle, with a tie beam right across at the bottom. This supports the roof very well, but puts the beam at a low level, cutting off all the space in the roof. Fine if this is a house, with a ceiling across under the tie beam, but not good for a barn where storage space is the whole point.

Other roof structures, like the hammer-beam, arch bracing, crucks *etc.* are attempts to give more uninterrupted space in the roof. Dorset had a really unusual and peculiar sort of roof, seemingly only found here – the sling-brace. These have only been found in barns, and even then only in barns where part of the wall is timber. Like hammer-beam roofs, they have tiny stubs where the tie beam would be, and are these braced by a timber strut which runs from a wall timber to a roof timber. Clearly this strange system worked because up to the 1960s there were eight barns surviving in Dorset with sling-braced roofs.

Two are seventeenth century (Holnest and Woodsford), and until the 1960s six more survived, all probably dating from the eighteenth century. Two of these have since been demolished. Barns at Bloxworth (New Barn, demolished); Morden (three, two surviving); Bere Regis (Roke Barn); and Tarrant Crawford: all had sling-braces.

Woodsford is really early, dating from around 1600 with the distinctive narrow brick, the earliest used in Dorset.

*Top right* The earliest sling-braces in Dorset in the barn of about 1600 at Woodsford Farm. The main rafters sit on a short horizontal beam which is jointed into a really weird curved upright. This upright is jointed bottom into a wall post and top into the rafter. The tie beam is a later insertion. Photograph 1949.

*Right* Barn of about 1600 at Woodsford Farm, Woodsford, with dwarf brick walls and timber above. A porch has been removed this side.

*Above* The seventeenth century barn at White House Farm, Holnest, in the 1970s before it was altered. Dwarf walls of stone, with timber above obscured on the left with an added building. The big porches either side had timber upper parts, like the main walls.

*Left* The roof of White House Farm barn showing the sling-braces – these are the slender, curving timbers centre background.

*Below left* Barn at Morden, neatly built of brick with a pantile roof, and timber panels in the upper walls. An isolated field barn away from anywhere. Dating from the later eighteenth century, it had the rare sling-braced roof structure. Demolished later twentieth century.

*Below right* One of the sling-braced trusses at Morden: the curved timber is the sling, bracing the roof rafter and the wall post. This was bolted together with iron bolts and strengthened with an iron band.

*Below & left*  The barn at Tarrant Crawford, stone below and brick of 1759 above. Inside, the barn has sling-braces: the wide medieval lower wall carries a much narrower brick wall. The timber wall posts rest on the old wall and carry most of the weight of the roof.

*Opposite page*  Detail of the wall at Tarrant Crawford – huge contrast between the neat, regular brickwork of 1759 and the much more picturesque fifteenth century stonework, with several different sorts of stone mixed with flint.

# Eighteenth Century

From the eighteenth century there is much more information on the barns, and the ways they were used. Many more survive as well.

Barns weren't just useful. The mad playwright John Pennie managed to wax nostalgic about even the barns at Lulworth. Looking back to the eighteenth century he recalled the old inhabitants who would

> boast of the dances that on winter evenings were so frequently held in barns . . . These rustic halls of ample dimensions, festooned, not with splendid tapestry of Arras, but hangings woven from the bowels of industrious spiders, and black with dust and age; round whose walls were displayed, not the blood-stained banner and dimly-gleaming panoply of warrior knights, but the peaceful implements of husbandry, were illuminated with numerous lanterns, suspended on a long waggon-rope passing across the beams. . . . the laughing villagers could see to dance their reels and jigs, eat their homely cakes, and drink their large brown jugs of lamb's-wool, which they always prepared of ale and roasted apples, to cheer them and their hired musician, who merrily scratched to and fro on the catgut of his crazy fiddle his horse-hair bow.

Twenty-five barns in one parish does seem too high a number, especially if they were all big ones. Pennie often exaggerates but he does give a happy picture of those 'rustic halls' being used for dances when empty of crops. Barns were also used by travelling companies of actors – the word barnstorming derives from this, and from the dramatic style of acting used.

Very occasionally farmer's account books survive. Samuel Crane of Bloxworth recorded the farm work in his diary, and the entries for New Barn in 1770 include thatching two ricks – one of wheat and one of barley at the barn, which was presumably too full of crops to store the sheaves inside, and then regular entries for threshing, *e.g.* 1st December 'Winnowed and screened 11 quarters and 3 bushels of Barley at New Barn'. Peas are also 'winnowed', and later in the year, oats. Crane uses the word

*Opposite page* Large barn at Belhuish, West Lulworth, dating from the early eighteenth century. This was built nearly ¼ mile from the farmhouse. Now used for timber work. The lack of doors in the porches gives a view straight through.

*Left* The roof of the barn at Belhuish, a simple 'A' frame, i.e. with collar beam across joined by metal bolts. Very neat timbering for tiles. Parts of the walls inside are lined with brick.

*Below* A plain early eighteenth century barn at Church Farm, Trent, with two big doors, but no porches. The neat loading hatches just under the roof and the side door are probably later additions. Modern grain silo left.

winnow meaning to remove the husk *etc.* from the grain.

Brick barns started to be built in the eighteenth century, looking just like stone ones in shape, size *etc.* The earliest is dated 1704 at Lower Lewell, and like several later eighteenth century brick barns, the date is worked in contrasting coloured bricks.

Rena Gardiner's illustration of the barns at Tarrant Crawford shows the change in building materials very clearly (see page 20). The lower parts of the walls of the right-hand barn are late medieval, maybe fifteenth century, and are a right old mixture of different sorts of stone and flint. These walls are wide. Clearly the medieval barn had fallen into decay, and probably even lost its roof. In 1759 the upper parts were rebuilt, but in brick and with much narrower walls. The roof was supported on the old medieval walls, using the sling-brace trusses found elsewhere in the county only with timber-clad walls. It was the narrowing of the walls which made this possible.

Hard chalk, usually called clunch, is too soft to be used as a sensible building material externally, but cheap and good for the inner face of walls. Many barns are lined with it, and because of its softness there is always graffiti. The huge barn at Shroton Farm is especially good, with many dates starting in 1731 on the inside of the walls which are completely of neat blocks of chalk.

Llewellyn Powys recorded some of this graffiti on clunch at Old Barn, Chaldon Herring:

> crowded now with farm implements, . . . [and] the white surfaces have been used by generations of Dorset labourers as tablets for the simple graphetai of their days. Many of them have been content with recording on the walls of their "fretted vault" a date and the initials of their names; other commemorate their loves either in valentine fashion by two hearts arrow-pierced, or more often by the grossest phallic drawings . . . One of the dates is as early as 1725, so that many of these primitive inscriptions must have been cut by men whose arms had been made strong by the swinging of mediaeval flails. The most common date scratched in is 1837, which marked Queen Victoria's accession to the throne; but 1830, the less happy year of the last labourer's revolt, also appears frequently.

One would expect large estates to build similar barns on all their farms: having worked out a suitable style, size and pattern it would be easier to repeat this. The earliest such group is found

*Above* Farmhouse with barn attached at Tincleton Farm, drawn for a survey in 1789. This rare record of a simple farmhouse and barn gives a good idea of an eighteenth century farm, although the chimney is a bit unrealistic. These buildings have since been demolished..

at Swyre Manor and West Bexington – early eighteenth century barns with distinctive very short porches on one side and copings on the gable walls with little finials. One very like Swyre Manor survives at West Bexington (opposite the Manor House) and there are similar barns with these very short porches at Looke Farm and Knapp Barn, both in Puncknowle. This group of at least five similar barns must all be on one estate.

In the north of the county is another set – three very closely related barns in Stourton Caundle, Bishop's Caundle and Caundle Marsh must all have been built at much the same time by the local landowner. Two have distinctive ventilation holes, and all three have probably original tiled roofs.

Dorset has few canopy-like porches – little projecting roofs with no walls. One survives at Brockington Farm, Gussage All Saints and there was another at West Stafford, on a barn dated 1776 in the Rectory yard. R. Bosworth Smith, a son of the rector at West Stafford, knew the barn in the mid-nineteenth century when:

> A stable and coach-house have been cut out of it, but it is still one of the biggest buildings in the parish, and looks as though it

could still hold a tithe of all the parish produce. The picturesque projection in the middle, under the shelter of which a loaded wagon can take its stand, extended its hospitality to all the birds … In these modern days [1905], a barn gives shelter, only or chiefly, to the uncomfortable-looking machinery, steam ploughs and reaping machines, which form the necessary stock-in-trade of the modern farmer; but, in my day, the barn was filled to the very rafters with wheat, or straw, or hay; and the dark recess in the topmost corner was the sanctuary of the white owl, which I would watch, while it was watching for its prey.

But the old barn had other uses than the agricultural. Parish memories clustered thick around it. It had celebrated, so I used to hear, the "accession of King George," probably of all the sorry lot of Georges, with equal and unquestionable loyalty; with better reason, the whole parish held high festival in it, "the young still dancing while the old surveyed," at the time of Queen Victoria, as it has, in later times, at her successive jubilees, and at the accession of her son. The first missionary meeting, which was ever held in the parish, was held beneath its rafters. One use to which it was put during the earlier part of the last century was highly illustrative both of the place and time. I have been told that scores of kegs of illicit brandy often lay, in perfect security, beneath innocent-looking heaps of hay or straw, till there was a convenient opportunity for disposing of them otherwise.

Barns were handy for smugglers to hide their booty, and for many other things. Right up to the Second World War they housed soldiers – even a cold barn was better than tents. There were very few barracks until the late-eighteenth century, so soldiers had to be billeted anywhere possible, and during the Second World War there were far too many soldiers for the barracks available.

Many very plain medium-sized barns seem to date from the later eighteenth century. They are found in stone, cob, brick, or a combination of brick and cob, and despite this variation in materials they are very similar in shape. They only have one porch, with just a wide doorway opposite the porch, and seem exactly the same size and type of barn a medium-sized farm would need. Although many (if not most) were built by the landowners for their tenant farmers, these barns look like the sort of sensible barns farmers would build for themselves.

Maybe the stone ones are the prettiest: Merry Hill, Abbotsbury, or the more severe one at Haydon. Turner's Puddle, is one of the most complete, built of cob with brick on the door surrounds and for the later buttresses.

ome are isolated like Merry Hill, some in farmyards like Bindon and some at a little distance from the main farm like Haydon.

*Opposite page* Early eighteenth century stone barn at Poxwell, the upper part of the porch of brick. An external sraircase leads to the upper floor of the porch. Demolished 1956. Photograph 1910s.

*Right* The eighteenth century barn at West Stafford in about 1895, when it was still part of the farmyard. The barn roof is extended downwards to make a cart shed, carts within.

*Below* The eighteenth century barn at West Stafford today. The timber framing with its brick infilling is original. It was converted into a house late in the twentieth century.

*Left* A barn defended: the later eighteenth century Poorhouse Barn at Wool was threatened by demolition in 1970, but thanks to protests like this one, it was saved, and has been converted into houses. It was called Poorhouse Barn because it was used around 1800 to house the parish poor, a workhouse.

*Below* The huge brick barn at Lower Lewell, West Knighton, dated 1704. Extended in the eighteenth century, the roof is still thatch today. The building has been restoed and is now offices.

Through to the later seventeenth century surviving barns are in the farmyards, close to the farmhouse and all other buildings. Documents show that there were isolated barns, but these do not survive. From the late-seventeenth century onwards there are many field barns – built right out in the fields, often a mile or more away from the centre of the farm they belonged to. They were sited close to the crops, which were stored and processed there, saving carrying the complete crop to the main farm. Surprisingly these barns are just the same as the ones built in the farmyard – one might have expected differences.

In the nineteenth century many of these field barns had cattle sheds added, and some even had cottages for the workers. A few became complete farms, but most were detached parts of another farm. These detached subsidiary farmyards are usually called 'out farms', and were unpopular places to live for most labourers because they were so remote. Many of the cottages have been demolished now, leaving the barn on its own.

Alone in the landscape, these barns can be very romantic. Llewellyn Powys was close to several at Chaldon Herring:

> Not far from my cottage on the downs is a barn known as the Old Barn. It is surrounded by a wall and there is a cow-pond within the enclosure. It is the very place for a man of philosophic temper to visit. It might have been built here on the bare hills for no other purpose than for human mediation. It resembles a diminutive Abbey Church standing within its garth.

This barn was mostly being used to store farm implements, and wasn't really needed in the 1930s when Powys described it.

Down Barn, Chaldon Herring, an isolated field barn built of flint and stone, probably around 1800.

The big early eighteenth century stone barn at Limekiln Farm, Castleton, with great porches and extensions tucked in. There are two more great porches on the other side, and the barn's 1970s replacement is on its right – full of straw.

*Above* The back of the barn at Shroton Farm, Iwerne Courtney, with the edge of one wing left, and the other much clearer in the background. Photograph 1970s

*Right* Inside the big barn at Shroton Farm showing the neat blocks of chalk used to line the walls. The roof is off.

*Below* The big barn at Shroton Farm dates from the early eighteenth century and is mostly greensand, with a little flint. The barn looks very wide because there are wings attached to the back. This is a very unusual layout for a barn. Photographed in 1953.

Distant view of Swyre Manor farmyard, with the big barn left, and other farm buildings right.

The big barn and farmyard at Swyre Manor.

*Above* The back of the early eighteenth century big barn at Swyre Manor showing the very shallow porch and loading doors right. It is remarkably similar to the large barn at nearby Berwick (opposite page), with coping stones on the gable walls and little finials. The porches are also very similar to Berwick, but here there is only one each side.

*Right* The gable end of the big barn at Swyre Manor, with the loading doors open: when unloading from a wagon, no ladder was needed.

*Below* Medium-sized, very plain barn at Swyre Manor. Maybe 1800. Rare external staircase foreground accessing another building.

*Above* Large barn at Berwick, Swyre, with extremely short porches this side, and huge ones on the other side. It dates from the early eighteenth century, but has coping stones on the gable walls, and neat ball finials like earlier barns. Modern (probably 1970s) grain silo foreground, but still straw in the barn, in huge modern rolls. Concrete ramp for loading manure centre.

*Below* The barn at East Bexington Farm, Abbotsbury, very plain and probably mid eigteenth century.

The barn at Merry Hill, Abbotsbury, is a classic field barn, isolated and well away from the farm. Typically it has a big enclosed yard in front, with one low animal shelter surviving. Probably mid-eighteenth century. The doorway is filled with netting hung on frames.

*Above* The loading doors at Merry Hill are set high in the gable wall, at just the right height for unloading a wagon.

*Right & below* Barn at Haydon Farm, Haydon, only 150 yards from the main farmyard. It is longer than Merry Hill Barn, but otherwise very similar. Built of thin slabs of local Forest Marble. Loading doors at the front. Probably late-eighteenth century.

*Above* Eighteenth century brick barn at White's Close,
Piddlehinton. Unusually it has the gable end to the street,
with odd triangular ventilation holes. Now housing.

*Above* Philliol's Farm, Bere Regis, all brick and dated 1748. It has one porch, and the thatch has been replaced. Dates on barns can be difficult to find, or very easy like this one.

*Below* The huge mid-eighteenth century brick barn at Roke Farm, Bere Regis, originally thatched. One of two original porches survives.

Sheep shearing at Manor Farm, Studland, about 1900. The wooden floor they are working on is the threshing floor.

The eighteenth century barn at Manor Farm, Studland, today. Stone and brick, with stone slates on the vast roof which extends down over the single storey outshots either side of the doors. Unusually these outshots extend beyond the doors.

*Above* Very small barns are hard to recognise, and have often been thoroughly altered. Vicarage Farm, Chaldon Herring, did have a big barn (now demolished) but this building in front of the house, is probably a tiny eighteenth century barn.

*Left* Remnant of an eighteenth century brick barn at Tarrant Hinton, cut across the line of the doors, when the main road was improved. Neat diaper decoration in dark grey brick, with chequering below. Tile roof with stone tiles at the bottom. The roadside cut has now been rebuilt in handsome brick.

*Above* Manor Farm, Bishop's Caundle has a vast late eighteenth century barn in the local stone, with a distinctive diamond of ventilation holes with pierced stone centre. Lovely tile roof. Photograph 1970s.

*Below* New Leaze Farm, Stourton Caundle, probably late eighteenth century and very like the barn at Bishop's Caundle, except that here the upper part of the porch is weather-boarded. The lower part of the door still has the cill. Photograph 1970s.

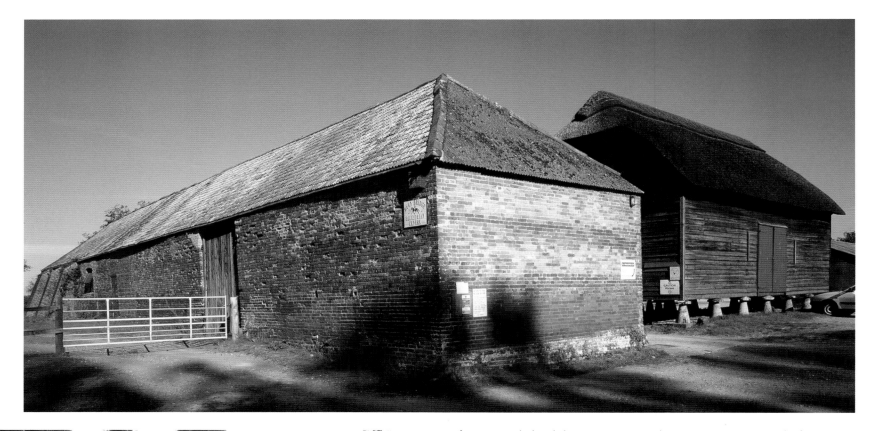

*Above* Simple brick barn at Hurn Bridge Farm, Hurn, typical of many in this area and probably dating from the eighteenth century. Granary on staddle stones right, and beyond this brick barn there is a cob one. There were originally two sets of big doors this side – the far set has been filled in.

*Left* Cob barn of medium size at Whatcombe Farm, Winterborne Whitchurch, with flint and stone dwarf walls, and still thatched. The other side has a huge porch. Probably late-eighteenth century.

*Above* Late-eighteenth century barn, Spring Garden at Turners Puddle: classic Dorset (outside of stone areas) with dwarf walls of brick, cob on top and thatched roof. The brick buttresses were added later. This is a field barn, well away from the main farm. The brick ends to the porch are probably a repair.

*Left* The roof of the porch at Turners Puddle has a simple triangular truss with a tie beam at the bottom, strengthened by a collar near the top. Most of the rafters (the smaller vertical timbers) are simply poles, still with the bark on. These 'natural' timbers can only be used with thatch.

*Above* Neat brick barn at King's Corner, Morden, probably late-eighteenth century. Big doors in the middle of the barn, and then a stable attached at the further end.

*Left* The diamond pattern of holes left for ventilation is unusually horizontal at King's Corner, Morden. Loading doors above.

*Above* Barn porch with 'canopy' extension braced by two stout timbers, at the Rectory, West Stafford. This brick barn is dated 1776, and survives converted into three houses. The porch is now much altered. The barrel seems to be propped up as a kennel for a dog. Ladders stored in the shelter of the porch. Photograph 1890s..

*Above* Brick and timber barn at Brockington Farm Gussage All Saints, probably late-eighteenth century. The little projecting canopy or porch with no walls is unusual in Dorset. On the other side there is a proper porch.

*Below* A medium-sized barn at Bindon Farm, Wool, built of the local very dark brown heathstone, in the mid-eighteenth century. The left hand building is the back wall of a cart shed. The farmhouse made the third side of the yard (on the right): it was demolished about 1950.

Medium size barn at the Elms, Tarrant Gunville, perhaps originally with a porch this side, replaced by dwarf brick buttresses. The barn was originally timber-framed above the flint and stone walls, now covered like the roof in corrugated iron. The large pieces of greensand probably came from the huge mansion of Eastbury, close by, demolished in the later eighteenth century. Barn probably late-eighteenth century.

Middle sized barn right on the road at East Holme, with dark brown heathstone etc. in the lower parts, and rebuilt in brick further up. This all probably dates from the eighteenth century. Weather-boarded granary tucked right up to the barn – and lots of communication – letter box, phone box and village notices on the door.

Late-eighteenth century barn at East Farm Dairy, Osmington, running right alongside the road, and with no porch this side, only big doors and three loading doors. This end is probably an extension. Probably eighteenth century.

Barn at Cross Roads Farm, Pulham, probably late-eighteenth century, with no porches and an accumulation of lean-tos at the back.

*Above* Barn at Kingswood Farm, Studland, very like the one at Higher Bushey. No porches, and the big loading bay in the gable has been blocked up. Probably later eighteenth century. Unusually the main door is towards one end.

*Below* Very plain barn medium sized at Higher Bushey Farm, Corfe Castle, probably late-eighteenth century with a modern roof. No porches, only big doors. 1960s barn beyond.

Sea Barn is isolated, very plain, all stone, and now thatched. It was built about 1800 and was beautifully restored in 1985, replacing a corrugated iron roof and repairing the walls. Little outshot addition left. Modern straw storage foreground – huge rolled bales clothed in plastic. No barn needed.

*Above* The gable end loading door at Kingston is most unusual: the builders have taken advantage of the rising ground behind the barn to allow loading off a cart directly into the top of the roof space of the barn.

*Left* Small barn west of Kingston, alone in the landscape, all stone with stone roof tiles as well. Big doors on the other side. Very difficult to date, perhaps late-eighteenth century, perhaps later.

Pixon Barn, Poxwell, out in the fields with its yard enclosed in front. All stone, dating from the late-eighteenth century. Typical big porch and high loading door. Modern storage background – silage in giant plastic bags.

High in the gable walls of many barns there is a hole, much too high and small to be useful. Often there is a ledge immediately under it. These are owl holes, placed to give owls easy access to the barn.

Josiah White remembered in his big stone barn at Whitecliff near Swanage:

> High up in each gable end was an "owl's doorway" about six inches wide and two or three feet high. One might think these openings were for ventilation only; but no, they were for the barn owl's accommodation. These birds were appreciated and encouraged in those early days, being good mousers.

Most surviving owl holes are much shorter than his two or three feet. Grain attracted rats and mice, so it made sense to encourage rodent-eating birds. The barn owl was the best of these. Bosworth Smith liked barns and the birds associated with them. In 1905 he wrote:

> Country landowners and their tenants, in old times were, it would seem, more alive than their successors of the present day, alike to their own interests and the beauties of nature, when, in building those picturesque old thatched barns which are still one of the glories of the more rural parts of England, they made a practice of leaving above the door and below the thatch, an "owl window" or hole to allow free ingress and egress to the winged friend of the farmer.

Smith had closely observed the barn owl:

> When left unmolested, as he ought to be, he becomes almost domestic in his habits, cruising around the rickyard or the homestead in search of his prey. The resort which he most frequents is a dark cobwebbed barn in which corn, or newly or badly threshed straw, is stored: for thither troop rats by scores and mice by hundreds, and there, ready for the farmer's greatest foe, is the farmer's truest friend, eager to destroy the destroyers. There he stands, bolt upright, perched on one leg, perfectly motionless, in some dark niche or on some lofty rafter, to all appearance fast asleep. But he sleeps with one eye or one ear open. There is a slight movement, invisible to the human eye, a slight rustle, inaudible to the human ear, in the straw below. In a moment he is all eye, all ear. The tucked-up leg joins the other; the head is bent forward and downward; the dark bright eyes gaze with an almost painful intensity on the spot from which the rustle comes. The mouse or rat shows itself, and in a moment again, without one movement of his wings and without one tremor of the air, he "drops" upon his prey. There is hardly a struggle or a cry; his long, strong, sharp talons – and no bird of his size has such long, strong, sharp talons – have met in the vitals of his victim, and he flies back with it, grasped tightly in them, to his coign of vantage; after a fitting interval of mediation, bolts or tries to bolt it whole, and then patiently waits for another rustle below. From such a retreat, well stored for grain and well garrisoned with rats and mice, he rarely, except for purposes of getting water, needs to stir.

*Top left* Owl hole with landing perch in the eighteenth century brick barn at Studland Manor.

*Bottom left* Owl hole with stone landing perch in the later eighteenth century barn at Haydon.

*Right* Owl hole above the loading door in the nineteenth century barn at Stoke Abbot.

*Opposite page* Unusual owl hole cut into the loading door at Spyway Barn, Langton Matravers, with a big landing ledge.

# Nineteenth Century

Barns were still vital in the first half of the nineteenth century, and the range of types is wider than ever. There are still even a few barns attached to their farmhouses, all under the same roof like the medieval longhouse. Rectory Farm, Winfrith Newburgh dates from the early-nineteenth century, and has house and barn under one roof. An American walking across Dorset in 1864 was shocked by the farmhouses and yards and saw

> a long, low building thatched with damp and mouldy straw, one half of which was the dwelling of the family, the other, the stabling for cattle and horses. The landlady of the inn where I lodged the night preceding, complained of this annoyance, saying that some of them were always ill from the odors of the cow-yard under their bedroom windows.

He was north of Bridport, having walked through the Blackmore Vale.

Agriculture was doing very well for most of the early part of the century and so lots of barns were built. Affpuddle has an extraordinary seven barns, two of them known to be of 1802, and five more very similar and of the same sort of date. All have brick dwarf walls with cob above, all had thatched roofs, and all were the same size. Four are in Affpuddle village or Briantspuddle, the other three out in the fields. Unusual to have so many barns being rebuilt, or newly built, at the time, but the barns themselves are typical, middle-sized barns of traditional form. They were built by the local landowner, not the farmers.

Bincombe is the other Dorset parish with a large number of barns of similar date, but here they are all of the local stone. There are at least five barns from the 1820s-1840s, two of them dated 1826 and 1827. Like Affpuddle, they are all of similar size, and they all have a single porch. Only the very latest one has two porches and uses a tiny amount of brick. These were all built by the landowner, a Cambridge college.

Most nineteenth century barns have some brick, often in stripes

*Opposite page* The barn at Home Farm, East Lulworth, is unusual in being built of the dark brown heathstone (with a little brick on the porch) and in being attached to the cottage.

with flint walling or with stone, and a few of them are all brick. These all-brick barns often have buttresses, like Blynfield Farm, Cann which is dated 1809. This also has very regular ventilation holes in a diamond pattern, much easier to do in brick because they are strong and all the same size.

Rather more barns with dwarf brick walls and timbering above survive from the nineteenth century, and there a couple of very sophisticated barns in North Dorset which have Greensand used for the corners and around the doors, paired with good red brick. This style is very unusual for barns in Dorset, and looks more like late Georgian houses. Church Farm, Motcombe, and Baker's Farm, Compton Abbas, are both in this style.

In the areas of good stone, brick was still shunned. Sometimes it was used to make neat arches over windows *etc.* as at Stoneleigh Farm, North Wooton, where a very unusual barn survives, a type usually found in the Lake District and Cornwall. They are known as bank barns, because they use the slope of the ground. The building is cut into the hillside so that the main barn is at ground level on one side for loading, but makes an upper storey on the other side, where straw *etc.* can be easily lowered to the cattle living there.

Cob is found much more commonly in the east of the county, around Verwood. There are many cob barns surviving in that area, most are smallish. These are difficult to date because cob went on being used in this area into the twentieth century.

This barn building boom continued in the mid-nineteenth century. Sidney Godolphin Osborne, writing of central Dorset in 1852, remarked on the amount of farm building. The landowners and farmers claimed poverty, but a visitor would not believe them because

> in every direction he will see large sums of money being expended on farm buildings on a scale and of a construction at once proving that the owners of property, however they may talk of despair, do not act it. Within an area of twenty miles around where I now write, I will venture to say more money has been expended within these six years in building new farm premises and improving existing buildings than was spent in forty years previous to the repeal of the corn laws.

The Corn Laws were repealed in 1844, so he is talking about a period of only eight years. Of course, not all this rebuilding was of barns – many cattle sheds were built at this time.

Anthony Huxtable of Sutton Waldron was a highly experimental farmer, and it is unsurprising to find that he built an experimental barn. L.H. Ruegg reported on Dorset agriculture in 1854 and when he visited Huxtable's farm:

> My attention was especially attracted by a large erection used as a rick barn, which I learnt was found of great service in "catching" harvest weather. This building, which was 40 feet long, 25 wide, and of considerable height, was composed of larch poles, wattled with furze, and roofed with half-inch boards covered with *brown paper* nailed on, and tarred and dusted with gritty sand four times. The run [fall] of the roof was 3 inches in the foot, and,

*Left* The barn at Tyneham, being transformed into the History Barn after sixty five years of disuse. Granary right. Tyneham Farm, like the rest of the parish, was evacuated in 1943 and never given back. Barn probably nineteenth century.

*Right* North Barn, Affpuddle, built in 1802, ¼ mile from the village across the meadows. Brick dwarf walls, then cob, and thatch. Photograph 1950s. Now converted into a house.

*Below* North Barn today showing the big enclosed yard in front.

*Above* Small and simple in Stour Provost, probably nineteenth century. Tall and rather narrow door at one end, rather than in the middle.

*Below* The gable end of a barn of about 1800 converted into Briantspuddle Village Hall. The granary next door is probably of a similar date.

notwithstanding the fragile nature of its covering, the high winds, which here sweep along with great violence, could not unroof it, nor the rain penetrate it. When it is considered that 1 cwt. of the paper, at a cost of 42s., will cover 2590 square feet of roofing, the extreme cheapness of this building may be easily estimated.

In fact tarred paper had already been experimented with in the eighteenth century and really it was not durable enough.

Barns were vulnerable to fires because generally they were filled with highly inflammable corn and straw. John Fisher, vicar of Osmington, wrote to the painter John Constable in September 1825:

> Do you recollect the situation of Talbot's barn behind the old Manor House, near the church, at Osmington? It took fire on 28th September, when it was surrounded by fourteen large ricks at the distance of no more than twenty yards. No water – no engines – straw on every side – the barn full of wheat – and thatched cottages and cornstacks in every direction. Talbot lost his presence of mind, and everybody was at fault. The occasion called me out of my usual indolence. I took command, gave plenty of beer and good words, worked hard myself, and in twenty minutes we smothered the fire, with no other loss than that of the barn. It was distressing to hear the poor rats squalling at one end of the barn as the fire approached them. They could not escape.

Wonderful detail, only preserved because the recipient became famous – sympathy for rats is unusual.

Converting barns into houses seems a modern thing, but occasionally it has happened in the past. The land agent at Bryanston in 1880 lived in a 'large, comfortable and commodious' house, 'very pleasant in appearance' which had been converted 'from one of those immense barns which once formed a very necessary adjunct to the farm'. This seems to have been done about 1840, and the building still survives as housing but is difficult to recognise as a barn.

Magiston Barn, Frampton, an isolated group of farm buildings centred on a big barn, probably early-nineteenth century. Unusual position for a loading door (right) and wonderful mixture of building materials (detail) in the barn at Magiston, including a pierced stone block used for ventilation.

*Above* Distant view of Blackmanston Farm, Steeple, set on a ridge in the big valley through Purbeck. The barn is just visible on the right.

*Right* The barn at Blackmanston Farm, probably early-nineteenth century. All local stone with a porch this side and big doors the other.

96

Cob barn in the centre of Verwood, used by the Cross Roads Pottery – their products spread over the yard on boards to dry. The barn (since demolished) was probably nineteenth century. Photographed about 1900.

The barn at Bower's Farm, Holt, has dwarf brick walls and timber framing above, with most of the walls covered with unusual upright timber cladding. Probably nineteenth century. Photograph 1930s, when it had the convenient sliding doors.

Hill Barn, an isolated field barn at Bincombe, dated 1826. In 1949 (above), it was being used for sheep-shearing. In 1956 the barn still had its wooden threshing floor. Today, Hill Barn is still in use and has a feed silo peeking over the barn.

*Above* West Farm, Bincombe, dated 1827. Modern roofing, probably originally thatched. Like this one, most of the Bincombe barns have original outbuildings attached.

*Left* Bincombe Barn, up on the ridgeway out of the village, dating probably from the 1840s or 50s. The big porch and the original outbuilding have some brick at the corners, otherwise all local stone.

The barn at East Farm, Bincombe, dating from the late 1820s or early 1830s, with modern roof.

*Above* Greenhill Barton, in Bincombe but away from the village. Like Bayard Barn, this is a farmyard with labourer's cottages, an out farm. All probably mid-nineteenth century. Photograph 1920s. Barn background right with continuous lean-to in front.

*Below* Greenhill Barton now, with the barn (left) having a big door on the other side, and more storage in the closer building

*Above* Bayard Barn, just in Bincombe parish, but miles from anywhere.
Barn background middle, dating from the early-nineteenth century.
Originally there was only farm cottages here, not a farmhouse. It was an
out farm, an outlying part of a farm.

*Right* The loading door at Bayard Barn is set very high in the gable wall.
Originally the barn was thatched.

*Above left* The large brick barn at Blynfield Farm, Cann, dated 1809. The buttresses supporting the roof trusses allow the main walls to be thinner. Probably originally without porches, as here.

*Above right* Rectory Farm, Winfrith Newburgh, a rare example of the farmhouse and barn all under one roof. This dates from the nineteenth century, probably early in the century.

*Below left* Small barn with big date – TF (Thomas Frampton) was proud of his barn of 1813 at Broad Lawn, Holt. The lowest parts of the wall are of heathstone. The barn is of 3 bays, and was originally thatched. No porches. Even smaller, timber-clad, possible barn background, probably early-nineteenth century too.

*Below right* Early-nineteenth century barns of traditional shape, with huge porches at Tolpuddle. All brick, and dating from the early-nineteenth century. These were two separate barns, with big doors opening straight onto the road, on the opposite side to the porches. Both now houses.

Compton Barn, Compton Valence, probably
nineteenth century and all brick. One end
converted into a house, incorporating one of the
porches.

A surprisingly sophisticated barn at Baker's Farm, Compton Abbas, of good red brick with stone corners etc. No porches, but a nice rounded arch one side. Probably built around 1810, but possibly even twenty years later. Shepherd's hut right.

Staddle stones were often used for granaries, but only rarely for barns, as here at Deer Park Farm, Wimborne St. Giles. The timber frame is held off the ground on the staddles: good for keeping out vermin, but difficult to drive wagons into. Probably early-nineteenth century.

*Above & left* Very symmetrical ventilation slits and squares on a plain stone barn with a very short porch. Converted into a museum for the local net and rope industries. Probably early nineteenth century, Uploders.

*Right* Symmetrical ventilation at Launceston Farm, Tarrant Launceston, in brick and probably early-mid-nineteenth century. No porches, just two big doorways.

*Below* Hampton Barn, Portesham. Isolated field barn, all local stone, probably dating from early-mid-nineteenth century. 1950s concrete barn left. No doors now on the old barn.

Spyway Barn, Langton Matravers is such a large and traditional-looking barn, its late date is a surprise – mid-nineteenth century. All local stone with stone roof.

Rempstone Barns, Corfe Castle – another farmyard of stone, probably
early nineteenth century, maybe a little later. Two big porches on the
barn. Converted into offices and workshops in 2000.

*Above & left* Greensand always makes buildings look older: a mid-late-nineteenth century barn in the farmyard at Manor Farm, Melbury Abbas, and a detail of the good stonework.

*Above*  The back of the bank barn at North Wootton, with the two high level loading doors, one with an elevator placed to feed it, worked by a little portable engine, tucked in behind. Barn probably mid-nineteenth century. Photograph 1970s.

*Right*  The front of the bank barn at North Wootton – the upper doorway is opposite the one at the back, but elevated. Cattle stalls and stabling below. Now a house.  Photograph 1970s.

*Above* Cob barn at Bramble Farm, Horton, probably originally thatched and very small. It has a proper big barn doorway, and a tiny window or large vent. The cob is being weathered away, having lost all its surface. Presumably nineteenth century, but hard to date.

*Below* Cob barn at Hope Lodge Farm, Horton, again very small but with proper doors and here a tiled roof.

Wonderful mixture at Coombe Farm, Langton Matravers, still with big doors, but much altered and difficult to date.

Barn doors usually didn't go right to the ground, but had horizontal boards across the bottom part. A farmer remembered:

> the peculiar pattern of the old barn doors in Dorset. The doors were always large enough to take a fully loaded wagon. The top parts of the doors were hung on each door post, but at the bottom there was no door at all, but a three foot high shutter in one piece which fitted into slots at the bottom of the doorway. The idea of this shutter was that the barn doors could be open to give light to the man inside threshing with the flail, while the shutter stopped the cattle from getting into the barn. They could, however, reach over the top of it, and I have often seen a crowd of fattening steers clustering round the barn doors, while the sound of the flail came from inside.

This shutter or cill is known as the threshold, and it is tempting (but wrong) to see this as the origin of the word – holding in the threshing.

*Left* Shutters in the doors of the nineteenth century brick built barn at Manor Farm, Milborne St. Andrew.

*Opposite page* Higher Barn, Abbotsbury, very plain and now lacking doors. Probably first half of the nineteenth century, and another isolated field barn.

*Below* Shutters still in place at the nineteenth century barn at West Hill, Winterbourne Abbas – planks held by wooden slots.

# The Beginning of the End

Mechanisation of threshing started in Dorset in the early-nineteenth century, and by the 1820s many farms had machines for threshing. These early machines were small and powered either by a horse gin, or turned by hand. They speeded the work up greatly, and did not need skilled labour – indeed at Bere Regis in 1810 a farmer found his threshing machine 'useful because it can be managed mostly by women'.

These machines, simple and small as they were, are the earliest mechanisation of barn work. The barn was still the centre of the work, and the machines were all housed there. The 1830 agricultural riots (the Captain Swing Riots) were partly caused by this machinery – threshing had been the main winter work for the labourers, and they feared losing their jobs. The rioters pulled the machines out of the barns, set fire to their wooden housings and broke up the iron parts. The machines were common – five were destroyed in Sixpenny Handley alone. Even these early machines could increase productivity by a factor of ten.

Some barns had small open-sided buildings attached to house the horse gin, feeding power into the barn, but many were used without any building over them. A few farms installed water wheels in the nineteenth century to power the machines, but this was not common because of the amount of work needed to feed the water to the right place.

Steam power was difficult to fit into existing barns. By 1854 there were at least 13 fixed steam engines on Dorset farms. The most admired was that at Bryanston which drove not only the threshing machine, but also a saw mill, bone mill (for fertiliser), chaff cutters, corn and cattle cake crushers and a malt mill.

Sometimes, as at Bryanston, these steam engines were housed in new farm buildings. They were expensive and most were bought by big landowners for their home farms, or by experimental farmers. The Rev. Huxtable at Sutton Waldron had one in 1854 and a writer admired

> The "tall chimney" and the extensive range of buildings stand in strong contrast to the surrounding downs, and light up with sudden activity and animation a somewhat desolate district.

*Opposite page* The eighteenth century barn at Roke Farm, Bere Regis, with the waterwheel of the 1890s which drove machinery in the adjoining building. Mechanisation like this helped make the big old barns redundant.

*Above* Barn at Berwick Manor, Swyre, in the early 1800s: a watercolour by John Baverstock Knight. Attached between the porches is an open-sided building to house a horse gin. The farmer at Berwick had a 4 horse power threshing machine in 1810, and this must have housed the gin and the four horses which powered it.

*Below* A horse gin at the Dairy Farm, Melplash about 1910. The horse walks round and round to supply power through the central gears. These were often used in the open air, as here.

These steam engines were state-of-the-art, but small capacity – Huxtable's was only 6 horse power.

There were never very many fixed steam engines in Dorset farms, and only one building to house one survives in its original state. The Buildings, Portesham was part of Portesham Farm, but well away from it. It looks like a factory, with a big chimney. A local remembered 'there was a beam engine with a squat chimney. This was used to drive a threshing machine and a small mill for grinding barley'. The farm belonged to William Manfield

The Buildings, Rocket, (now Portesham Farm) Portesham. A very rare example of a set of farm buildings (including the barn) designed around a fixed steam engine (chimney centre). Proper barn door (left), with rounded arch. An out farm, probably mid-nineteenth century.

*Above* Chimney added to the seventeenth century barn at Manor Farm, Silton, to vent a fixed steam engine which powered all the jobs in the barn. Chimney early-mid-nineteenth century.

*Above* Diagrams make things clear – machine threshing in 1866 – traction engine powering an early thresher, fed directly from the ricks, which are up on staddle stones.

*Below* The enemy of the barn on the move – a traction engine pulling the big threshing kit at Chilcombe, about 1914–18.

who was a well-off landowner and farmer. He promoted the Abbotsbury Railway, and seems to have been just the sort of experimental farmer to build this steam-powered farmyard. The Buildings was probably constructed in the mid-nineteenth century, when a fixed steam engine was the best solution, but these were soon made obsolete. Interestingly The Buildings had a surprisingly conventional barn.

The chimney added for a steam engine survives at Manor Farm, Silton: in the nineteenth century this area was owned by the Sturts of Crichel and in 1854 'the tenantry on [the Sturt] estates are said to have been the first who themselves bought fixed engines for threshing, winnowing *etc.*' The Silton steam engine was used up to 1890 and dismantled in the 1930s.

Traction engines, steam power which was movable, started to be used in the 1860s, and dominated from the 1870s. They too were expensive, and usually hired along with the threshing machine. A whole winter's threshing could be done in a couple of days. The old corn barn was redundant – with machine threshing it was much easier to keep corn in ricks in a yard where the machinery could be set up – a rick yard, or stack yard.

These traction engines were versatile, and could be used for ploughing and many other jobs as well as threshing.

A succession of storage at South Field Barn, Sydling St. Nicholas, an isolated collection of farm buildings. Late-nineteenth century barn left, modern steel-framed next (probably 1950s) with a later feed silo, and open storage of straw in big rectangular bales right.

Rare conversion of a barn into a terrace of four houses (instead of the usual one) at Church Farm, Child Okeford. The brick barn originally had two sets of sliding doors: big recessed areas are clear either side of the doorways. Barn later nineteenth century.

Barn at Wynford Eagle, fronting right onto the road. Plain flint walls with brick corners etc. Probably later nineteenth century.

Unusual barn at St. Mary's Farm, Chettle, with no buttresses. Windows have been added very neatly, probably in a new upper brick wall on original flint lower wall. Nineteenth century, but difficult to date more accurately.

Barn with dwarf brick walls and timbered above at Dene Farm, Sixpenny
Handley, probably nineteenth century, but possibly a bit earlier, now with
a lantern over the end.

The remains of an isolated field barn at Watcombe, Alton Pancras, overlooking the village of Plush. There was a cottage here in the mid-nineteenth century, so this was an out-farm. The surviving buildings are mid–later nineteenth century. Amazing that the loading door survives.

Isolated New Barn at Maiden Newton, shown on the map of 1888, and probably very new then. The wide panels of flint and sliding doors are typical of late barns in Dorset. The windows high up may be original. The photograph on the right of one of the ventilation slits at New Barn shows the good quality of the brickwork.

Isolated barn at Greenford Lane, Wynford Eagle, mostly of rather brownish brick, but with stone in the very lowest parts of the walls. Mid-later nineteenth century. The detail of the wall shows the neat ventilation slits, and how the brick has eroded.

Unusual barn at Stoke Abbot of the local stone, with some brick. The tiny 'windows' for ventilation are odd. Very difficult to date, but probably nineteenth century. Detail of one of the ventilation 'windows' – these are arranged symmetrically with two on each long side.

In the late-nineteenth and earlier twentieth centuries there are a few photographs of barns actually being used.

*Left* A proper farmyard at Tory's Barton, Turnworth in the 1890s. Big barn (background left), with cattle and hens all over the yard – the half barrels are for cattle feed. Granary right. This barn and granary now demolished: another big barn survives.

*Below left* Rare view of sheep-shearing inside the barn at Monkton up Wimborne, 1941. Dwarf brick walls and wood above.

*Below* Wagons full of apples ready for cider in one of the barns at Upton Manor Farm, Uploders, about 1912.

*Opposite page* Drove Farm, Tarrant Gunville, right up on the chalk, a huge set of farm buildings in very rough flint and good brick. The barn (right) is a relatively small part of the complex, and has sliding doors fitting into recessed panels (all brick). Shown on the 1880s map, but new then, perhaps 1870s.

# The Latest Barns

Proper barns weren't needed in the late-nineteenth century. A handbook on farm buildings of 1889 is severe:

> In the process of altering and improving homesteads, it will be found that the barn is that part of the buildings which more often lends itself to a useful alteration . . . Farmers when they complain that they have not sufficient buildings on their farms, do not realise the fact, which is often the case, that if the barn space was properly applied to modern requirements there would be little to complain of. When a suggestion of interference with this ancient institution is made, it is not always approved; but you can thatch corn or straw, or cover it cheaply in Dutch barns in the stackyard, whereas you cannot thatch your cattle or implements. Landlords originally supplied barns for the purpose of threshing corn in by hand, and there is no reason at the present time why they should be provided, or allowed to stand as such, if required for other purposes, except so far as one, or a portion of one, may be required to house a few loads of straw in a handy position for chaff-cutting or litter.

The old barns, these 'ancient institutions' continued to be used, but Dutch barns were the future. These open-sided barns start to be built in Dorset in the late-nineteenth century. They had been known in England from the seventeenth century, but they only became common when mass production of the steel frames made them cheap. The barns were used to store anything, but hay was the commonest. Earlier, hay had always been made in ricks, thatched for protection, and this of course continued. The hay in the rick or Dutch barn was not baled because this was not possible until well into the twentieth century. The hay was piled into the rick or barn loose, and it packed down into a very dense hay which had to be 'trussed' into bales if sold off the farm.

A few traditional barns were built in the late-nineteenth century, or more likely rebuilt after fires. Insurance paid for the rebuilding. With mechanical threshing barns lost their main function but in 1872, a Dorset farmer explained that 'Barns are almost as necessary as ever, if not altogether applied as in old times'. On model plans for farms published in journals, barns are usually

*Opposite page* A huge barn at Fiddleford, since demolished, steel framed with corrugated iron over much of its sides. Probably late 1930s.

*Above* Dutch barn near Blandford, probably 1900-1910, with typical curved roof, but with wooden poles rather than a steel frame. Eight mowers with scythes to cut the hay. Lots of hay already in the barn.

called 'straw barns' from the 1860s, used to store the straw after threshing.

Dutch barns were virtually the only ones built in the twentieth century, with steel or reinforced concrete frames. These were mostly pre-fabricated, ordered from the specialist firms, and identical all over the country.

Some simple pole barns continued to be built, usually quite small and often using redundant telegraph poles as supports.

Barns had always been used for dances and suppers, and we get many more records of these extra uses from the nineteenth century. Concerts became much more common, and reached even small villages. Stoke Wake had its first ever formal concert in January 1888, held in a barn which was 'very chastely and prettily festooned with evergreens and chains of coloured paper, whilst numerous mottoes decked the walls, giving it almost the appearance of a ball-room.' They were trying to stop it looking like a barn.

At Wyke, one of the huge sixteenth century barns was used for a harvest home Thanksgiving service in the twentieth century: 'a section of the barn had been cleared, and bales in the manner of the pews of a church, with a central aisle.' This was in the 1960s, celebrating the simplicity of the barn rather than hiding it as at Stoke Wake in the 1880s.

At Lytchett Matravers 'the Tithe Barns were fine specimens of the kind and although their former use was obsolete, the buildings have come in very usefully for much needed parish rooms.' This was done about 1860, formally changing the rector's stores into a village hall.

*Below* Dutch barn at Margaret Marsh, with complicated uprights and an extension supported on timber poles. Probably 1930s.

Some Dorset barns were used as theatres – Tyneham rather informally about 1900 with 'a rough stage' and hired chairs. Plays and pantomimes were staged to make money to build a village hall. The seventeenth century barn at Wytherstone was also adapted into a theatre in the 1930s.

Gore Farm, Ashmore, has a very rare 1920s barn. The old buildings were burnt down in 1928, and Rolf Gardiner rebuilt a traditional barn, of local brick, flint and timber with a 'fireplace of baronial proportions'. The barn was used by the farm but also as the centre for work camps and meetings, and had a huge rough candelabra and brackets for candles. Now fully converted into a house, Gore Farm must have been the most unusual barn in Dorset in the 1930s with its huge fireplace.

Some barns were still used to store corn in the mid twentieth century – John Eastwood worked on the harvest at Burton Bradstock in the late 1940s and was

sent to help out "down barton", This means standing on shifting sheaves on the wagon and throwing them up with a pitchfork to Tom Gallon, who stands on a half-built bay inside the great barn. He, in turn, passes them to old Charlie, who is up in the dim heights of the barn, "laying" the sheaves. He works quickly, on his knees, keeping the inner wall straight and true.

The last loaded wagons come in and are unloaded. At nine o'clock we stop work. Now the barn is almost full; tomorrow we will have to build a new rick in the yard.

John wasn't trusted to arrange the sheaves in the barn: this skilled task needed old Charlie.

Since the 1990s there have been a few modern houses designed to look as if they were converted from barns, and several new village halls which are very barn-like. Horton's timber-clad hall (2009) looks just like a medium-sized barn, even having big doors in the side.

Many of the old traditional barns have been demolished, some have been converted into housing or even offices, and many are still in use on farms. Some, including even a few of the early barns, are in poor condition and have no purpose.

Barns in Dorset are a combination of geology and farming, simply part of the landscape. They are under appreciated and often ignored, even in parish histories, but the idea of a barn is often used to represent traditional rural life and values. Dorset barns are superbly varied, and still common. They deserve our appreciation.

*Top* Pole barn at Clarkham Cross, East Chelborough, with corrugated metal sheeting this end, and unusually for a barn, guttering and a down pipe. Filled with big rolled bales of straw wrapped in plastic. Later twentieth century.

*Above* Barn with steel (left) and reinforced concrete frame, two different phases, both late twentieth century, Warren Farm, Puddletown.

*Left* Concrete framed barn, Roke Farm, Bere Regis, built in the 1960s.

*Above*  Barn at Stinsford, just off the A35, very like the one at Buckhorn Weston, but with a later extension this side, and concrete walls added to make it into a silage bunker. The silage is covered with plastic held down by tyres, and some big rolled bales of straw parked on top.

*Right*  The maker's name plate on the barn at Stinsford (Leominster is in Shropshire). There don't seem to have been any Dorset manufacturers.

*Far right*  The roof of the barn at Stinsford, very lightly constructed in steel, is a great contrast to timber roofs.

*Above* A recent barn at Waddon Farm, Portesham, very different from the earlier barns, but still providing storage for farming.

*Opposite page* Traditional Dorset barn at Whitcombe with its new golden thatch. Originally built in the seventeenth century, the barn was carefully restored in 2008. Church behind.

# Notes

### Introduction

Josiah Dorset White, *Reminisces of English Country Life* (n.d. *c.*1925) pages 21-22;

William Saint (1864 – 1934), Recollections, mss. Dorset County Museum;

John Pennie, *The Tale of a Modern Genius* (1827) page 182;

R. Bosworth Smith, *Bird Life and Bird Lore* (1905) pages 235-236.

### Medieval Barns

Barton Farm, Cerne Abbas: John Hutchins *History ... of Dorset*, 1st edition, vol. II (1774) pages 281 & 292: 2nd edition vol. 3 (1813) pages 295 & 316;

H. J. Moule, 'Cerne Abbey Barn' in *Proceedings of the Dorset Natural History & Antiquarian Field Club* vol. 19 (1889) pages 186-191;

same author, same title, same journal vol. 22 (1901) pages 62-67;

Thomas Hardy & the barn, in Herman Lea, *Thomas Hardy: Through the Camera's Eye* (1964) page 29;

Abbotsbury security contrivances, see Ship Album no. 2 page 87, Dorset County Museum;

Sherborne – Hutchins, 2nd edition, vol. 4 (1815) pages 98 & 99;

Tarrant Crawford – Hutchins 1st edition, vol. II (1774) page 45;

Cerne Abbas barns – Hutchins 1st edition, vol. II (1774) page 292.

### Tudor & Seventeenth Century

Sir Frederick Treves, *Highways & Byways in Dorset*, 1906, p341.

*From Victorian Wessex The Diaries of Emily Smith*, 1836, 1841, 1852, ed. Margaret Smith (2003) p 41.

### Eighteenth Century

'boast of the dances' John Pennie, *The Tale of a Modern Genius* (1827) pages 183-184;

Bloxworth, Anthony Blad, *Samuel Crane 1746-1815 Dorset Farmer* (1999) pages 20-23, plus information kindly supplied by Tony Blad;

'a stable and coach house' R. Bosworth Smith, *Bird Life and Bird Lore* (1905) pages 228-229;

'crowded now with farm implements' and 'Not far from' Llewellyn Powys, *Somerset & Dorset Essays* (1957 edition, original publication 1935) page 169;

The lithograph of the three barns at Tarrant Crawford is by Rena Gardiner and is from *Dorset: Tarrant to Blandford* (1970)

For the amazing barns being built especially in newly-enclosed or reclaimed areas see *Georgian Model Farms* by John Martin Robinson (1983). These are much grander than anything in Dorset.

### Owl Holes

'High up in each' Josiah Dorset White, *Reminisces of English Country Life* (nd *c.* 1925) page 21;

'country landowners' R. Bosworth Smith, *Bird Life and Bird Lore* (1905).

### Nineteenth Century

'a long, low building' Elihu Burritt, *A Walk from London to Land's End and Back* (1865) page 180;

'in every direction' S. G. Osborne, *The Letters of SGO* [1888] edited by Arnold White, page 51;

'My attention was' Louis H. Ruegg, 'The Farming of Dorsetshire' in *Journal of the Royal Agricultural Society* vol. 15, part II no. XXXIV (1854);

### Thresholds

'the peculiar pattern' W. C. Smart 'Seventy years of Dorset Farming' in *Dorset County Journal* vol. 1, September 1946, page 23.

### The Beginning of the End

'machines managed by women' & 'machinery at Swyre' William Stevenson, *General View of the Agriculture of Dorset* (1815) pages 157 & 149;

Jill Chambers, *Dorset Machine Breakers* (2003) pages 20-21;

'"tall chimney"' & 'Sturt tenants with steam engines' Louis H. Ruegg, 'The Farming of Dorsetshire' *as above*, pages 410 & 402;

'there was a beam' Anon, *Under Black Down – The Story of Portesham A Dorset Village* (1968) page 13;

the Silton steam engine, see *Silton Records of a Dorset Village* (1983) pages 73-74.

the traction engine and threshers, see R. A. Whitehead, *Steam in the Village* (1977) with lots on Eddison's, Dorchester. See also Peter Stanier, *Dorset in the Age of Steam* (2002) pages 17-23.

### The Latest Barns

'In the process of altering' A. Dudley Clarke, *Modern Farm Buildings Their Construction & Arrangement* (1899) pages 38-39;

'Barns are almost' Joseph Darby, 'The Farming of Dorset' in *Journal of the Bath & West of England Society* 3rd series, vol. IV (1872) page 39;

'very chastely and' *Dorset County Chronicle* 2 February 1888;

'a section of the barn' Description of Wyke, quoted in *The Living Village* by Paul Jennings, pages 57-58;

'the Tithe barns' Notes on Lytchett Matravers by Florrence Carré, page 76, Dorset County Museum;

'a rough stage' Lilian Bond, *Tyneham A Lost Heritage* (1956) page 8;

T. P. Connor, *Wytherstone: A History of a Dorset Settlement* (2010);

'fireplace of baronial' Rolf Gardiner, *Water Springing from the Ground* (1972) page 103.

'sent to help out' John Eastwood, *Life in a Dorset Village* (1982) page 65.

# Acknowledgements

Both David Bailey and I are grateful to the farmers, landowners and owners of the barns included in this book. Without their support and encouragement it would have been impossible to even attempt a modern illustrated book about Dorset's barns. We lack the space to list them all by name, but that does not lessen our debt. Many thanks to everyone.

I knew that Dorset barns were varied, and that little research had been done on them, but it wasn't until I was well into working on this book that I realised quite how varied and complicated they were, and how small the amount of work done on them was. Dorset barns deserve more research than I have been able to do, and this is very much a first attempt at looking at them.

This book would have been so much worse without the Royal Commission on Historical Monuments' work in Dorset – both the published volumes and the original recording for the entries in those volumes have been vital, especially for the barns up to the early-nineteenth century. It was the RCHM investigators who discovered the unique Dorset sling-braced roof (indeed they had to invent a name for it). Several of their photographs are used here, and many others have been used during the research. Dorset is so lucky to have been completely surveyed by the RCHM, and to have the investigator's records so readily available from the National Monuments Record. Our thanks for supplying the records on so many Dorset barns.

Of course, this book does not properly reflect the relative numbers of barns of different dates in Dorset. Only one medieval barn has been omitted; half of the surviving sixteenth and seventeenth century barns are left out. Less than one-third of the eighteenth century barns we have located are illustrated, and there must be many we have missed. The proportion used is even smaller for the nineteenth century, and for the twentieth century there are just a few barns to represent the hundreds in the county.

We have looked at over 500 barns and taken photographs of most. These photographs will eventually go to the Dorset County Museum. We were biased towards those that were visible from the road or path.

We are grateful to Tony Blad; Peter Press; Jeany Poulson and Johnny Read for help with Dorset barns, and to Tony Bradshaw for yet again saving us from many errors, and much information. Thanks to David Bailey for his superb photographs, and for suggesting a few barns.

The acknowledgements above are in the plural because Christopher Chaplin (my husband) has done so much of the work. We criss-crossed the county looking at barns, but many were found by him on solo cycle rides. He kept control of the huge amount of data and photographs we generated, and has critically word-processed the book – very argumentative typing. He says the work was therapy after serious surgery, but for me it made the book possible.

All the illustrations are by David Bailey, with the following exceptions: Blandford Museum, page 136 top; Christopher Chaplin, pp. 31 top right, 36 bottom right, 76 bottom left, 78 bottom, 104 bottom left and right, 133, 137, 138 all, 139 bottom left and right; Country Life, page 58; Dorset County Museum, pp. 4, 9 top, 12, 20 top, 31 top left, 33 all 3 in black and white, 39 top right, 40 bottom left and right, 47 bottom, 49, 53 top right and bottom left, 59 top, 60 top, 63 top left, 72, 75 both, 81 top left, 98 bottom, 99 top, 102 top, 1113 both, 121 bottom, 122 bottom, 132 all; English Heritage/The National Monuments Record, pp 29 centre, 32 bottom, 40 top and bottom left, 50 top, 51 top left and bottom right, 52 top, 63 bottom, 91 top; Merle and Alan Graham, page 30 bottom; the late Rena Gardiner, page 20 bottom; Yale Center for British Art, Paul Mellon Collection USA/The Bridgeman Art Library, page 18.

*Jo Draper*, Dorchester 2010

*Above* Idealised Dorset field barn, drawn in the early 1950s showing the barn with its yard and lower buildings for cattle. Shepherd's hut left. From Ralph Wightman's *The Seasons* (1953).

Out-farm at Chideock, Chaldon Herring.